"The poems in *Everything is Rising* are vivid in imagery and deep in emotion and nostalgia. Diane takes you to places that you may not want to go, but you are a better person by having been there.

    -Barbara Marie Minney, author of *If There's No Heaven*

"Memory is the mother of all wisdom" according to Aeschylus. Such sagacity stirs in *Everything Is Rising*. Using what the poet calls "the fossil of my voice," she distills the past's influence, waking us to a world where "blood tastes like creation." Let these pages carry you with a pulse that "has never beat gently" and on "into morning light."

    -Laura Grace Weldon, 2019 Ohio Poet of the Year

Also by Diane Vogel Ferri:

Fiction:
No Life But This: A Novel of Emily Warren Roebling
The Desire Path

Poetry:
Liquid Rubies
The Volume of Our Incongruity

Everything is Rising

Poems by Diane Vogel Ferri

Luchador Press
Big Tuna, TX

Copyright © Diane Vogel Ferri, 2022
First Edition: 1 3 5 7 9 10 8 6 4 2
ISBN:978-1-952411-98-4
LCCN: 2022934595

Cover image: Martha Vogel
Author photo: Lou Ferri
All rights reserved. No part of this publication may be reproduced or transmitted in any form or by any means, electronic or mechanical, including photocopying, recording or by info retrieval system, without prior written permission from the author.

ferripoet@gmail.com

Acknowledgments:

Grateful acknowledgment is made to the editors of the following journals who first published these poems:

"In the Center"	*Braided Way*
"Ephemera"	*Poetic Sun*
"Why We Are Here"	*Poetic Sun*
"Daughter"	*Poetry is Life*
"Lines"	*New Verse News*
"Requiem"	*American Journal of Poetry*
"Mother"	*American Journal of Poetry*
"The Houses"	*Her Words- Black Mountain Press*
"How to Leave"	*Her Words - Black Mountain Press*
"I, WASP"	*Dissident Voice*
"Ebb and Flow"	*Aurora and Blossoms Poetry Journal*
"American Dream"	*Wend Poetry Journal*
"For You"	*Blue Heron Review*
"Look Up"	Lyrics for the song "Look Up" Music by Ryan Charles Ramer (Cleveland Composers Guild)

Table of Contents

I.

Sycamore / 1

Wonder / 2

Daughter / 3

Son / 4

Prolapse / 5

For You / 6

Little One / 7

Dancing / 8

The Houses / 9

Her Story / 10

Me Too / 11

Larceny / 12

In Absentia / 13

A Mother's Day / 14

How to Leave / 15

Folly / 17

Everything / 18

II.

Buckeye / 21

My Father's Gift / 22

The Trees / 24

Gone the Sun / 25

Eternal / 26

I Will Sing for You / 27

Ephemera / 28

Familial / 30

Words / 31

Vapid / 32

Requiem / 33

Uprising / 34

Ravenous / 35

The Calling / 37

The Boy Who Couldn't Walk / 38

Mesmerized at the Beach / 39

September Song / 41

Death on a Playground / 42

The Running Girl / 44

Unforgotten / 45

Distracted / 46

The Twins / 48

The Gift / 49

When I Leave / 50

III.

American Dream / 53

Bequeathed / 54

Mother / 55

Respire / 57

Monarchs / 58

Interlopers / 59

Ode to the Glaciers / 60

Yosemite / 61

Grand Canyon / 62

The Great Lake / 63

Greta's School Strike for the Climate / 65

Stillborn / 67

Extirpation / 68

Understory / 69

Survival / 70

Quietus / 71

A Good Eye / 73

Autumn / 74

Infinite / 75

Look Up / 76

The Sex Life of a Lightning Bug / 77

IV.

Sudden Symphony / 81

Missing / 82

Insipid / 83

Blunted / 84

Surreal / 85

Subliminal / 86

Quarantined / 87

Why / 88

Lines / 89

I, WASP / 91

Incantation / 93

Praying Mantis / 94

Apart / 95

Sound / 96

Ascension / 97

In the Center / 99

Plenty / 100

Emergence / 101

After This / 102

V.

Collective / 105

Torn Heart / 106

Sublime / 107

Another Day / 108

Gratitude / 109

Meditation / 110

Final Flight / 111

Until We Meet Again / 113

The Speaker / 115

Simple Stories / 116

Ebb and Flow / 118

These Children / 119

Why We Are Here / 120

For Lou

Good art originates not from the desire to show off but from the desire to show yourself. Good art always comes from our desperate desire to breathe, to be seen, to be loved.

-Glennon Doyle, *Untamed*

I.

A time to tear and a time to mend, a time to be silent and a time to speak.

-Ecclesiastes 3:7

Sycamore

Can you smell the sweet
when we walk by

our hands clasped
like the past

can you see the bark
weeping off the trunk

peeling down vulnerable
like a naked lover

can you imagine
branches like spider legs

crawling across the sky
older than our time

can you recall
when we were undefended

when there was no weeping
before we could smell the sweet

Wonder

I said to the little boy
this is where I grew up,

I am trying to keep it
but it is a butterfly out of the net.

This is a song I knew,
but you don't have to listen,

you have new songs
that come out of your hand.

I am loping along next to you
as you dart away like a sunny day.

You wonder how I knew your papa,
how we were once friends,

how I was ever young,
when I knew more than you.

We run to the back of the yard
to swing and dance,

we find stones for a treasure box,
fish we will catch and then let go.

Daughter

When you slid out of me
you were already holding her
in the dark cave of your belly.

She languished until we could not
do without her, could not live
in this lonely place any longer.

Her bones are lengthening,
gathering in the world
with all of its words and gestures,

her fearlessness is all the beauty
we need today, all the kisses
we can catch in our open hands.

We three are knit together
with the sun and the moon,
brimming over the ages,

never still, never the past,
always tomorrow.

Son

The world has spirited you away
as it is wont to do,

you slipped out of my hands
down the river through

the woods into the light,
son in the sun,

an oracle sailing on a light breeze,
a runner of fiery pulse.

You look like all the ages
before you, your silhouette

passing through the miles
and years as you and I buried

the dross to find our shared spirit.
I watch you with your little boys

in your dragon arms
carrying my dreams with you.

I see you are a safe place for them
and I am skinned to the bone.

Prolapse

I think about being a woman now
more than I ever did before,

about small indignities, slipping down,
my bones being slivered from me.

I think about the fossil of my voice,
the doggerel of my language,

the trench coat I wear in the world
to protect my blended scars.

I think of how my female duties have
been faithfully and willingly fulfilled,

how only words remain to explain
the inadequacies of recent years.

I think about unsolvable mysteries, like
how I got this far into the future, the

sudden lure of cemeteries, why we are
stealing the world from our children.

Then I remember my unencumbered
life, how my senses are still striving.

I want to hone myself into a new being.
I need a kiss to re-inflate my lungs.

For You

i'm like a pencil sketch now
faded, gray, yielding

on yellowed fragile paper
in another unwanted reinvention

i walk into morning light
as dreams crawl off my shoulders

my body like feathers
my feet flat and steady

muscles peeling away
except the pulse of heart

it has never beat gently
into the night for you

you can't see me but I will stretch
like a shape-shifter for you

walk across the crooked river
swim the eerie lake for you

i will swallow the wrongs
like a heron

taking the fish whole
for you

Little One

I know how you feel, little one
when you repeat your demand over and over

and I do not understand what you are saying
you move close to my face and speak louder

and I say *I don't know, I'm sorry, little one*
you are frustrated and undeterred

but eventually you grow
weary of the futile fight

you turn away from me
go back to your toys and books

you have already learned
how it feels to be unheard

Dancing

I was a carefree little girl who loved to dance
across the living room to *West Side Story*

like a glitter-winged fairy, loved to flip and cartwheel
in my gymnastics uniform until my body became the show,

not my performance. It was hard to prance in a slouch,
so I put colors on canvases until the art teacher said

I didn't have his devotion to art and he painted over
my work. I taught children, then, on a first date,

a man told me he wanted to take care of me forever
as if I was unable to care for myself.

I changed my name, but couldn't exist as
mrs. husband's name—always left off of the envelope,

so I liberated myself, un-obliterated myself.
An older gentleman wanted to teach me to dance again,

he said, *You must let me lead, do what I do,
feel me guiding you,*—but I could never follow.

The Houses

Too young married, too young a mother
to babies who slept in a room of budding mold,

without the security of insulation
in a tiny pink petal of a house, near water

that unfurled its lake effect in winter and
papered the rosy siding with insects in spring.

The neighbors were thorny and shot bb guns in the yard,
so we plucked the babies and fled to grow a new life

out of leaking radiators and rotting wood on a
crooked framework, but with lilacs that unfolded

over the front porch like a garland in May.
I opened each morning with a blushing smile

for the one who should have remained a friend,
and lived out my good-girl prospects.

I nurtured and loved as I wanted to be loved
—atoning for as long as I could, then

I emerged like a rose in late December
blooming into the new year.

Her Story

This girl, this bird who sings, she remembers everything.
-Roseanne Cash

She laid out the memory that changed
everything, every sunrise,
every decision, in the body, in time,

in the car parked in the driveway,
the phone ringing, the changed address,
muted for decades, still growing,

unseen and secret, rooted below the skin
while they denied her truth, twisted her reality,
excused the accused, the lucky unharmed.

She laid out her story neither left nor right,
neither death nor resurrection, just that which
marked one day from a lifetime;

the galloping pulse, the sewn-up lips,
untethered flinching that is part
of every girl, acknowledged or not,

public or private, believable or
unconvincing, in the nadir of a burden
to be worn like a cape all of her days.

Me Too

In your perfect childhood you don't know
your body will not be yours for long,

but to truckers whooping as you walk home
from school, to grown men who will say what

they want as you hunch your shoulders
and ruin your posture. The shape of your body

weighs you down and you cannot hide it in a
gymnastics uniform, you cannot sing on a stage,

you don't know if your voice will be heard,
and you soon learn it is not your choice.

At your first teaching job, every morning
the principal will look you up and down,

comment on your outfit, every afternoon
stand at the doorway and stare, interrupting

the children, your work, your dream,
your reason to be there.

Larceny

Here is
a word temple
of how it happened:
You took my virgin tapestry
and poked a menacing hole into it,
a larceny that time will not mend, it's a photo
I carry inside my sleeve, how the sky smothered
us when we were searching for the crooked river.
While you
were speaking in
tongues I was looking over
the edge for a savior, and that's
what I found, for a minute, standing in a
different galaxy, crucified, bleeding, open and waiting
on that island, while you waded in, greedy, empty, hungry.
You tried
to drown out your
iniquities with golden liquids,
the click and fizz sounded like the overture
of an opera to you, music you would lick off
the table or suck out of my mouth if I let you, and in my
purity, I let you, I was like a zebra mussel suctioned to a rock.

In Absentia

Here is a glass of words that would not exist if you had not
put the damage on my existence. It calcified, limned with
lipstick stains and subliminal messages. The
words would have been mutable,
possibly non-existent,
if not for your cruelty,
the blood-stained,
fraudulence
of it all.
I will
not
fault
you
for
your
sins,
for
without
you the
poems,
the eternal life,
the glistening gift of
my future would have been impossible.

A Mother's Day

You feel like a mermaid, young
and lovely, but bound at the ankles,

you caress your tough external scales
but feel the oozing inside, your wilding paused.

Former loves are engraved on your skin
but out of reach: the music and mayhem,

the moshing and self-love. You can't hear
the higher callings bleaching the air,

but there are two spirits at work here
in the tangled curls and bruised foreheads,

the winter-born, the summer-born
beauty that you birthed.

One day the marathon will be
in your peripheral vision, in the annals of time.

You will be unfettered,
but may long to be a mermaid again.

How to Leave

My mother couldn't be an artist
because it just was not done,
        not by mothers
               who had better things to do

who put on lipstick and combed their hair
while the roast was in the oven
        when shirts
               were dancing in the breeze

on the backyard line and children
came home when streetlights lit up.
        But one year
               my mother disappeared

to classrooms filled with easels and paint
the attic was emptied of broken toys and
        outgrown clothes,
               a hole cut in the roof to

let the sun in, and where there once had
been darkness and decay there was light,
        where there had been
               emptiness there was

delight, a whole person where only half
had lived for years bundled up in those eyes

   that saw what no one
     else could see, hands

moved deftly across a canvas filling the studio,
proving that we can be more than one thing
   showing us how to leave beauty
     when we're gone.

Folly

My mother wanted to keep me because
two others were unborn before me,

so she took a drug to save me, and
I was saved, but not because of the drug,

God just had mercy on both of us, I guess.
When I was fifteen she read that the drug

was giving girls cancer. Red-faced,
horrified, she informed me that I

must go to her doctor. Guilt-ridden,
my mother wanted to know if I would

still be a virgin after the examination, she cried
at what she had done trying to save me,

but did not blame the folly of the doctor
who caught me on my birth day.

Everything

you never stop being a mother
with your shriveled belly-skin
and bleeding breasts

you chose to wound yourself
and the bruises just keep coming
don't they?

it's really
the only thing you are
that never goes away

you may stop being someone's wife
or someone's teacher
but not someone's mother

they think you don't remember
the day they came out of you
their first day of school

you may be quieted, weakened
but you remember
everything

II.

Even in laughter the heart may ache, and joy may end in grief.

-Proverbs 14:13

Buckeye

the memorial tree we planted has
begun to yield its glossy buckeyes

fresh out of their capsules
in the shape of the deer eye

grown in midwestern glory
on its propagating continuum

the branches have stolen the view
from our front window

but not our memories
of the one who is not here

the rest of us are growing old
with our stories that stretch

longer with each season
and our wonderment

at the brevity of it all

My Father's Gift

Before our last Christmas together
my father drove to the CVS

at the top of street I grew up on,
because that was as far as it was

safe for him to go after
seventy-five years of driving.

He might scrape the side of the
garage when he returned,

or maybe it was my mother
who misjudged and knocked

over the garbage cans. But he
had pulled my name out of a hat,

so he had shopping to do.
He bought a metal lantern and a

comforter with a blue and green design.
With shaking hands he wrapped them

as best he could and on Christmas Day
I opened a gift of two things

I will never part with.
Then we hid the keys upstairs,

the stairs they could no longer climb,
in the house they built sixty years before.

The Trees

I glared out of my upstairs bedroom window
at my father and his father--cigars hanging

from their mouths, beer bottles set in the shade,
the Indians game on the transistor radio--

as they chopped down trees in the front yard
to make room for a garden that would never

bloom, clearing space to hit a baseball or fly a kite,
to flatten the yard and plant more grass to mow.

My crying and pouting had not stopped
the atrocity, had not stilled the saws

chewing through the small trunks
of the trees that never had a chance to grow up.

I don't remember ever being angry with
my father before or since that day. I knew he

loved the trees, raking the piles to burn
in the ditches, or dump at the end of the slide,

he loved the radiance of autumn beech leaves,
the land he and my grandfather had cleared

to give us what he had taught us also to love;
the trees, the land, our life there together.

Gone the Sun

for my father

When will I remember you living
> not still
when you gave us Yosemite and oceans
> and piles of leaves

When will I remember you wise
> not silent
when you sat in the car with me
> telling me there would be other boys

When will I remember you bolder
> not smaller
when your arms were the strongest
> your legs the fastest

When will I remember you peaceful
> not tormented
when the days were not built
> on a hill of pain

When will I remember you breathing
> not breathless
when I was your partner
> and we won every game

When will I remember your songs
> not a soldier
in a strange place with a bugle
> playing day is done

Eternal

for my mother

The colors of heaven are in the trees
this early November afternoon.

Last year you sat in the chair where I am
now, overcome with the yellow and red.

After eighty-six autumns
you never wanted to come inside.

What is your heaven now? Do your
seasons change in the light-filled glory

where you live on without me, without
your paintbrush and your chalk?

You left behind the beauty
for those of us still waiting here.

Your body doesn't hurt when you paint
or play the piano now, you don't need help

up the steps to your studio or out of my
porch chair. You are not gone,

but survive in my love of beauty, in the
work of your hands that covers our walls.

I Will Sing For You

You are laying still, broken, expendable
in a metal room of erupting sounds

applesauce shoved into your mouth drools
down the front of your gown day after indecent day

ministers come but you cannot swallow the wafer
and your blinking has no answers

I am afraid to touch you even though
I came out of you, afraid of your beseeching

Then I heard you singing, saw you dancing
(the sun had to be soaring through the windows for the dance)

At the piano we sang together,
I can hear it, I can see it, can you?

I bring the music, sing all the songs
for you and your eyes never leave mine

but when the music is over
you are too

Ephemera

That house is not alive
it is dead trees and earthen bricks

the once here and now
is the past with wounds

she died in the living room
on the bed of the last stranger

he was stolen to the wrong building
alone and never to return

soon new babies come in the back door
and slip through life just as we did

fences and walls sprout up
unsolicited photos push into us

and we say how wrong it is
these living hallucinations that won't go away

we try to keep that century animate
to honor the rooms of conception

for the ashes in the yard
of the house that ate us alive

for the carving in the soft bark of
a beech tree we couldn't dig up

the roots too strong
too deep

Familial

It is a loss
when someone leaves your life,

even when the deprivation is not
about forgiveness or death,

but about what we can no longer bear:
vitriol, jolts, the profusion of words

that leave a perennial disfigurement, like
the zipper-wound of a scalpeled heart surgery.

Estrangement feels wrong when
we see each other in a nonpartisan place

so the damage is sustained,
like the deep scar on my withered hand,

the one that should have been sewn closed
because I was trusting with a knife,

even though our mother and father
taught us to be careful with sharp things

when we were children together,
didn't they?

Words

I took it on my shoulder and lugged
it like a saddle, an unseen wound.

I held it in my breath and tried to exhale,
but all I could do was inhale.

I gasped at the scar it was leaving so I
cut off my ear, but your tongue kept moving.

I exported the information to disperse
past communication, and imported the new.

Like a dump truck, I hauled your words
into a fire that just keeps burning.

Vapid

The bell jar broke and I was vapor,
steam from a tea kettle, gray fog,

when you left me off the list,
out of the yearbook again, your

no reply was oppressing. When
we met, my face made me feckless,

a dull flower in a dreary garden.
At the bottom of your trash heap

I saw the unread pages of my book,
which wiped me away. Inconspicuous

as a sparrow, I curled in the barren dirt
like a November leaf, undetectable

in brown rubble, something to be
sent to a more fruitful garden.

Requiem

H
e
r
e
is
the
church
here is
the steeple
open the doors
see all the people
as they fly to a galaxy
far far away where they
have new red feathery bodies
and watch over us earthlings and
send us good luck and at Christmas
they hang on the shiny tree while we trash
their time here on this planet and reduce it to a locket
in a jewelry box, a framed moment in time, a song we knew
in childhood, a little money to buy something useless, all
meaningless because the church doors are closed and there
are no more people to visit on Easter, or care if God is dead
or alive, there are no children in Sunday school
or vacation bible school, no children to sing Jesus loves me
this I know.

Uprising

Who will see it
        if not me
who will break out
of these shriveling days

I bite my tongue
        and feel
that I still bleed and the
blood tastes like creation

I snap dead
        blossoms
off the flowers recalling
their orgasmic glory

I kneel and dig
        for more colors
until my fingers are buried
my vision increased

I pull myself up from
        the nadir
I don't comply I inspire
I don't wither I rise

Ravenous

On icy Sunday mornings
I throw buckets of seeds and mealworms

out on the deck just to watch the coexistence.
From behind the slate sky browns/grays/black/

white/red-crested/ the complimentary blue-orange
of the eastern bluebird arrive.

The winter has silenced their songs
but not their need.

I used to sing in a flock of sorts but now there is a
cemetery in my throat, the loft is empty and

my inglorious cords have devolved
to the sound of the geese barking across the pond.

God must be taking pleasure elsewhere
on Sunday mornings, silence being only a venial sin.

When I was a child and had a nightmare, I'd open
my mouth but nothing would come out,

I would wait in the dark for my voice to return
to call for comfort as I do now.

Outside there is no soaring contralto of the wren
or murmur of the starling in this bleak midwinter haze,

just the circle of hunger as a quiet congregation lines
the deck rails waiting for their turn
                              at the sudden sufficiency.

The Calling

I am quarantined in the silence of my back deck,
but for the caw of crow, the scree of hawk,

the chip-chipping chickadee, until
the *zzzhawing* of a power saw chews its way

through the morning, cutting into the quietude.
When it mercifully stops I hear two voices

behind the wall of woods calling for a lost dog.
The child's voice moves away, the man's comes closer.

I cannot see them as they call in echo form,
one then the other in a hopeless rhythm.

I think of my Stella, vanished on an ordinary day,
how I panicked, shouting, imploring, beseeching,

until I found her a half-mile away, calmly sniffing
where her nose had taken her from me.

I come back to the calling in the woods
as it falls away into the distance

until all I can hear is despair
threading itself through the summer air.

The Boy Who Couldn't Walk

The boy was locked and loaded in a whirring machine,
maneuvering through scarce choices hidden in the day,

bucking the abandonment of a body, the one that
wouldn't move on demand; the brain and muscle detached.

All that was broken was stitched into every moment,
despite the love and devotion of a father

who left himself behind somewhere in his dusty youth,
waiting for every call in the night like a soldier

who can never sleep in battle, in the cold, lonely foxhole
of fate, in the holy war pact they could never reverse.

We didn't know how the boy would break free
of his shackles, but were left with a vague vision

of a heavenly stroll on another plane,
walking, running, with the dog who went before him.

Mesmerized at the Beach

unknown child under water
my gaze fixed until he comes up

then my eyes search for
who is watching this little boy

as he emerges open-mouthed
gulping hazardous water

the wind and waves are raging
jet skis cut like knives

no one will hear his calls
but me ~~

I look to the children
for everything I am

all of my life
sister, mother, teacher, grandmother

my eyes love every child I see
my ears love every child I hear

but it is too late to repair
decisions I made long ago

the ones that made
the children cry

they assault me now~~
rising from heavy dark waters

a wave finally swallows my towel
as I watch the boy run

out of the danger
he will never know how much I love him

I taught children with special needs for over thirty years…

September Song

It rained outside
and inside the little boy said,
I smell the rain because I'm like a dog.
I'm feeling pale today.

The little girl said,
I can't have summer vacation
anymore and that's why I'm crying.
We all cry for freedom, but

it is in the past and we are
in this century-old brick building
swimming in withering humidity
preparing for tests before the children

have had a chance to learn anything.
My soul cries for the innocents,
for the stomach aches and tears,
for the broken pencils and scattered

scrap paper, and for the boy who
left the room in his humiliation
and abandonment
never to return.

Death on a Playground

In memory of Tamir Rice

The newspaper unfolded
in the innocent light of morning,

to the impish grin of a child.
The one who sat in my classroom,

in math class, shouting out answers,
escaping to the hallway, crying

like a large toddler, too tall,
so happy to see the adults

come running to his rescue.
His mother in the school office

telling us he was a good boy,
and he was —

under the lost, unsafe days
moving from school to school,

the new boy, new classroom,
wanting to be known.

He craved attention,
so one day he got it

with a toy gun on a playground
and a bullet in his side.

The Running Girl

She barked like a dog,
and hid under her desk

when it was time for math
because math was a bad dream,

as it was to me when
I was eight, so sometimes

I crawled under the desk with her.
The foster-mother visited

the school for her
good children, but not this one,

this one ran out of the
classroom as I called for help,

the foster-mother turned away.
A building in chaos, searching,

a missing child found in the lunch room
calmly eating her lunch.

Month after month we chased her
until the foster-mother adopted her,

the running girl changed her name,
and stopped running.

Unforgotten

I've forgotten the names
and faces of hundreds of children,

but not the child who screamed for help
every time I opened my mouth to teach him,

or teach the quiet ones, or utter anything
to get us through the humid afternoons,

in closet-like spaces until we could
touch the fresh silent air.

Nothing was learned or gained
in those months when this child,

a ward of the state,
was included, as the law demanded,

as he called for someone to rescue him.
Plan after plan faltered and failed,

because we were not the right people
to save him, we were not a family.

Distracted

It took *three* seconds for his eyes to avert,
his head to turn—one day I timed it.

So every *two* seconds I marked the paper
on his desk with a star, a reward

for briefly defeating the lead in his blood,
in his brain, the poison no one asks for,

but is given freely to the undeserving, a future
of failure for being born in the wrong place.

My pointed index finger was invisible
as it slid down the page in front of him,

the words I uttered were inaudible,
my face incomprehensible.

This child never needed a chair because
he would dance by his desk to silent music,

a show for the others,
some entertainment to delay the progress

until the bell rang, until the scheduled
meeting to report the data, the sad story

to tell—this boy has not learned
anything, all year, on any day,

and the mother said,
I won't give my boy drugs.

The Twins

One twin was the guardian of the other,
although no one taught him how to do that.

Blood and a mysterious dyslexic haze
bonded their underdeveloped synapses

across a landscape no one else could see.
Their mother couldn't count coins,

the numbers just didn't add up.
Their father argued with paramedics

who came to take one breathless boy away.
We shuddered, we adults, the liars,

helpless as seven-year olds, trying
to save him from hearing his daddy's

refusal of his safety, while the other boy cried
please bring my brother back—day after day,

alone in his darkness, shut in an illiterate haze,
stifled and stymied by disorder and birth.

The words made no sense.
The separation was agony.

The Gift

I ask the children to wait,
not to leave like the others

for they have restored me
like the waves returning to shore.

They are not mine to keep,
so I stretch my arms out,

reaching in their direction
over miles of punishing riptides.

Every blink they change,
so I close my eyes to see them.

I arrive with a basket of graces;
see someone in the window,

hear my name around the corner,
dogs bark, cats run.

My stretched-out arms
cannot hold it all, bring it in,

my back cannot bend enough,
so I just take the gift.

When I Leave

My lips are dry from kissing
the top of your head, your pink pillow cheeks,

my arms are light from their sudden rest
but strain empty all the same,

and my back has told me about
all the lifting and holding it has done today.

I am still singing that nap-time rhyme
into the yellow-white curls on your neck

wondering if this will be the last time,
the last rocking chair song.

III.

But ask the animals and they will teach you, or the birds of the air, and they will tell you.

-Job 12:7

American Dream

I heard the bees clustered
in the garden, and felt the hammer

of their sting on my bare feet.
I saw the bat wings furious in the streetlight

and felt the carbon of the stardust
pouring down through the moonbeams.

I stole daffodils and lilacs from
the exalted fields and brought them

to my grandmother, five houses down.
I went to the beech trees glowing yellow

in the fall, the scritching of metal rakes
uniting them in bountiful piles.

I laid down in the dandelion grass
to look up at my life as I wished

it always to be, where the sickle thrashed,
the sheets dried in the wind, where

I heard the whirr of the push mower,
where, undoubtably, we had it all.

Bequeathed
(for my grandchildren)

Here is the world we are giving you—
one we don't understand but inexplicably cling to:

a world of apathy and ardor, delusion and truth,
turmoil and the peace of wild things.

You will discover that dreaming isn't real
and that tears and amniotic fluid never run dry,

that time changes everything
and anything can be a weapon,

that God is not a man but just love, and
this revelation will carry you through your wandering.

Someday when your knees will not bend you will
tear up these words of wisdom and write your own,

you'll wonder why we didn't do better on this
ruined planet, this sphere of paradise and hell

and why we couldn't stop ourselves
from passing it on to you,

someday you will.

Mother

I

Mother loved me, gave her whole self to me,
so I fracked her, cracked her, broke her,

chopped her, bit into her, dumped garbage
on her until she turned an unearthly, neon green.

I piled my stuff on her until the excess
tipped over, spilled into the future, into her

grandchildren's playgrounds. I lit fires
and fanned the flames, burned her clothing

and her dignity. I was like a cicada frantically
chewing my way through my short existence;

mating, consuming, trashing, desecrating
the very thing I worshipped. Yes, Mother

loved me, gave her whole self to me, but I bullied
her until she had no choice but to end herself.

II

I loved Mother. She was the only home I ever
knew. I grew up with her, lived with her,

all my memories are of her. I exist because
of her, but she suffered a prolonged febrile

death and I did nothing, gave nothing
to save her.

Respire

I remember what it's like not to breathe,
the riptide in my lungs, the terror as oxygen

leaves the extremities in an underwater
dream, all going black, blank.

I watch the back yard flooding.
Someone else's lawn chairs

gliding by like small whitewater rafts.
Now its seeping into the basement,

fear is rising as an iconoclast sits
in the skeleton trees laughing at the

drowning refugees, the soggy, ruined
treaties, the caskets skimming

down the streets, the sludge of the poor,
collapsed colonies, the smell of rot.

We used to know how to swim but
another torrent is coming. How do you

swim in the oil creeping up to your
house, how do you breathe?

Monarchs

Somewhere
monarchs
are alighting in the trees
like wildfire
I want to catch them
on my tongue
hold them in my arms
safe from the confusion
and the damage
we've bequeathed them
consuming the delicacy
of their wings
as if they are worthless
devouring their colors
cursing the milkweed
sending them helplessly
into the burning woods
along their inherited path
obliterating
beauty

Interlopers

You weren't here when people
worshipped the stars, when their

moccasins left no footprints,
when they bled together and

nature was their mother, when they
spoke to the trees, grew out of their roots.

Look at the centuries and now
this moment of misinterpretation

and avarice, we are interlopers of the earth.
The artists toil and suffer to preserve

the richness of culture, tradition
and pride, gifts for those to come.

You weren't here when it started,
you won't be here when it ends,

but other living-breathing may be.
And you won't be here when their

children play in a graveyard,
a world they didn't bury.

Ode to the Glaciers

They are licking the sea,
drooling like helpless babies,

coming out of eternity's
hibernation in loud wailing,

their saliva obliterating the path
of the penguins, happy feet

pattering on their home of soggy
sea ice, intact families, the

father sheltering eggs under
his body for months while the mother,

after dropping her babies in a puddle,
wanders for food that resides on the

underside of the solid water, soon
the fuzzy chicks are hopping then

dying when their march is over, never
knowing water was their enemy.

Hear the ice cracking, see its tears,
touch the warm forehead of its fever.

Yosemite

We went to Yosemite
and it was a dustbin

we strapped on our
breathing masks

covered our noses
from the stench

covered our mouths
from the shock

we visited singed grapevines
traipsed through ashes

and towns with billboards
thanking firefighters

for saving their lives
but not their beauty

El Capitan rose through
the smoldering clouds

Half Dome stood valiantly
stubbornly in the valley

smog cleared from the mountains
then we could see it all

Grand Canyon

we had seen the canyon looking like art
unexpected snow nestled into its crevices
crowds rushing to turn their backs and
take a photo never stopping to look
we had traveled 2000 miles to see the stars
in the crushing black, my small pupils couldn't
take it all in, my insufficient mind couldn't
contain the galaxies of ancient light
I didn't gaze as long as I should have
because it was so cold without the sun

The Great Lake

The messenger slid haphazardly
down the enflamed river

and wrote the shameful plea:
Help me, I'm dying (signed) L. Erie,

of industrial waste, fertilizer run-off,
sewage, filth, belly-up walleye,

smallmouth bass, their dead mouths
now gaping large, cluttered the shores,

wallowing in the rockin' 70s pollution,
from gilded gluttony, wounded by greed,

the onetime great city reduced to a
late-night joke. So it was rescued

from imminent death, the woeful graffiti
stared us down during the painful rebirth

while we heard the siren of our labor pains,
saw our mistakes on the lake. Now revived

beaches are strewn with humans in cleansed
air, music, trucks of food, people littering

the shores, rowers gliding the guilt-free
serpentine river, jogging our memories.

> * *In 1969 the Cuyahoga River which flows into Lake Erie caught on fire and Cleveland became a national joke. The graffiti Help me, I'm dying. L. Erie appeared on the 55th Street pier in letters so large they could be read from the highway leading into Cleveland. This led, in part, to the Clean Water Act of 1972.*

Greta's School Strike for the Climate

She cried all day at school, no eating
or speaking, howling panic attacks

heard round the world from the girl
who asked --why are you teaching us about

plastic in the ocean then boarding a plane?
Blindness and stasis are not alibis so she

walks directly into the fear, taking her sign
to the streets. She asks passersby to take

a photograph and post--and post. Fridays
are not the days for school or indifference

but for truth. Suddenly everyone wants to
help the waif-like girl. Mean children,

bullies want to be her friend although
children have never been kind before.

Then the crowd becomes thousands.
She cries, she panics, she stays.

What have you given up for the children?
she glares into the room of strangers,

when have you looked past your own life,
past this morning? It is not worth the time

to talk to the ignorant, the blind. Just film
this speech and send it throughout the world.

Stillborn

The numbers are slipping off the clocks
as our muscles stubbornly vibrate.
Newborns travel here looking for light,

oxygen, reaching tiny hands out to touch
the trees, but the ash borer took them, the
unwelcome visitors, coincidental consumers.

I take the babies to the water
and cower at the dust in the river,
stripped of fish, then search the trees

for eggs to crack open while we are
plowing a trench through their someday.
The massive hole we are digging

is ugly and moldy and not ours to dig.
We cut and steal, slash and scorch and
teach the babies that if they play with

matches they will burn the house down, with
all those precious embryos gasping for breath,
how will we explain it when they are stillborn?

Extirpation

Why should I care what leaves,
what it will take with it?

Like the horns of the northern white,
the West African, and the Sumatran rhino,

the haint blue of a macaw, the
brilliant golden light of a toad,

the stripes of a tiger, the slimy trail
of the Hawaiian snail, the mouse-like

creatures who drowned on their own island.
Diversity will be shrunk to the back

yard where there is no grieving process,
so we'll stuff them, lock them behind glass,

un-dignify their existence, insulting the
God who made them. What we lose is

everything: the differences, the efficient,
unparalleled creation we once worshipped.

Understory

spray the ants and watch them drop like flies
chase the squirrels away from the bird feeder

rip the hook out of the fish jaw and
throw his body back to where it came from

angrily sweep the sparrow nest out of the
bluebird box because you want blue not brown

crush the stinkbug against common advice
letting it rot your fingers for the day

make someone else pick up the dead bird
under the living room window or cry doing it

shake the goose eggs or drench them with oil
for being such a noisy nuisance

poison the unwanted growth, the natural, that is,
until everything is perfect, the way it's supposed to be

then sit motionless for the beautiful heron
as it painstakingly stalks the frog-less, fish-less pond

Survival

The birds in flight
bring gifts as they slant

across my view, land
in the trees to pray, sit on

cold, silent eggs. The bluebirds
sound like Mozart, the wren calls

day and night for a lover, the bard
owls go a-courting in the dark.

They will not be silenced, because
survival is all they can do.

I want to crawl inside their silver
feathers, rise up into the air

with them, look down, see what
they see. Maybe we can still cross paths

with a condor or a bald eagle.

Quietus

I am stopping now,
to listen to silence,

to watch the squirrel
take an improbable leap,

to see sun-shadows,
the dog lying in gleaming

grasses, ears erect to
sounds I cannot hear,

her neck stretched tall,
eyes scanning her domain.

She knows how to stop.
How can I explain

to the little girl
why the silence is

temporary, why the
cicadas will scream in

the stripped trees,
why we can see the moon

in the daylight, how the earth
is not here to amuse us

but sustain us, how
I wish I could dive into its

interior and re-inflate its lungs
just for her.

A Good Eye

I have been like the little bird
with one good eye.
As I moved to the feeder
to refill the seeds
she didn't see me.
So I poked her purplish wing
once, twice.
She hopped about to face me
with her one good eye
then flew away.

Even with two good eyes
I have only seen half
of what can be seen.
But year by year
my callow vision improves,
like veils being lifted away
one by one or
like a foreign language
that sounds like nonsense
until you learn it, speak it
understand its beauty.

Autumn

The trees are about to drop their shade,
their hiding places, their majesty, for

another colorless sleep, in their eternal
faithfulness of the great plan.

I smell delicious burning leaves in my dreams.
I see my father laboring, hear the scritching of his rake.

I remember the fear of fire in ditches
and trying to keep the children safe.

I look out my own back window now,
but see the endless yard of my childhood;

the metal swing set, the tether ball,
the heap left for us to jump in,

someone at the window
watching, the earth spinning, infinity.

Infinite

How many birds have touched that tree,
the one that fell in the storm,
snow heavier than its branches.

How many years did it grow its rings
and how many wood chips will it make
to carpet the barren ground.

How many days will we be here
watching the evolution of these trees,
the deer nibbling on the lower twigs,

the black and brown squirrels chasing,
coexisting with the gray ones,
so reminiscent of God's original plan.

How much do I love creation
and the cold beauty of earth,
always waiting for a renewed season.

Look Up

Pull your eyes away
from electronic interlopers.
Stave off all urgent replies and forwards.

Gently lay your burdens down
as a baby enveloped in a crib
of blankets and soft comforts.

Guide yourself out where
the humid winds move through you
like shape-shifters,

and the spring peepers
noisily mate in the twilight.
Look up, look up.

Don't wonder how it happens
every night of your life.
Don't say it's beautiful.

Say nothing at all.
Forsake the moment.
Disremember the day.

Look up, look up.

The Sex Life of A Lightning Bug

The flash is only the beginning—
until the nuptial gift is revealed in a shiny coil

to be accepted or rejected—here the female
has all the power, all the choices,

she waits it out for the protein-rich,
never aware of her biological clock.

Our sex life includes the cherry stem you tie with your
    tongue,
although knees and backs won't always bend and hold.

Wildfires to the west, hurricanes to the east,
storms in the snow belt, can't end the allure.

Nature changes as we have—you are my lightning bug,
a luminaria—or a tiny night-sun, a star I choose to live on.

IV.

*You will not fear the terror of night, nor the arrow that flies by day, nor the pestilence that stalks in the darkness, nor the **plague** that destroys at midday.*

-Psalm 91:6

*In 2020 the world changed with the arrival of the Covid-19 pandemic.

Sudden Symphony

small waves of dread
coursed through me
intermittently

when I thought about
the coming months
the distance of my love

I walked the streets
with all the others
heeding our spaces

when I looked up
the sky was bluing, widening
when I looked down

the grass was greening, living
when I invited them
the birds were a

sudden symphony
the never-changing
had arrived

Missing

Violet sees me in the tiny rectangle
and shows me the dimple on her right cheek

she doesn't yet know that I am of some
relevance to her future and I am ineffable

I am a face that gawks and waves
I am a voice that says *there's Violet!*

and I wonder if I can at least teach her
her name if I say it enough into the void

I appear and disappear like the sun
climbing through scattered clouds

a useless beggar of time
a thirsty lover of babes

her sister flits in and out, pushing
her blue eye or her red-gold hair

against the screen hello and goodbye
we will play in the summer

and I am bereft of their silky skin
and the weight of their body on mine

Insipid

I burrow even deeper
into the minutiae of the day

like a fox looking for a dark den
a frog nestling into the mud

to find the achievement
in opening cupboards

and tossing out expired food
—-the wastefulness of it all

I search for the mindfulness
in a load of laundry, a clean floor

I crawl in even deeper afraid
I won't be able to drag myself out

that this is what a rampant virus
and my common sense can give me

and I won't be able to forgive myself
for where it has taken me

muddling around in weak-willed hours
staring out windows, seeing nothing but beauty

Blunted

Do I love life enough now
the mindful breaths and steps

intermingling joy and indifference
why do I open my fists sometimes

and let go, dropping from the heights
into dank cold blankness

crying and wine send me to sleep
but do not keep me there

at night I descend into a gaping maw
where people used to be

people I thought would miss me too
I see now that was an illusion

I try to sing but weakness strangles my
throat decayed in disuse

I watch food lines around the parking lots
trail of tears in this uncontrollable wildfire

zooming in on my wrecked heart
trapped behind an open door

Surreal

It's all schadenfreude now
a finger in the eye

God crying with that knee
on your neck

we'll just plow through this
these evictions and endless lines

bullies win the day
deniers win the year

clocks are draped over branches
elephants are on stilts, a torso is missing

we old ladies have nothing to say
so old white men explain it to us

identities disappear
like eyelashes, waists, and pink lips

so we put on our bullet-proof vests
then puncture the children's futures

with our silence and watch
the evil twirl their mustachios

the last supper has arrived
as we watch the ship of fools floating by
                            we must be in a Dali painting

Subliminal

it has infiltrated my roots
        so I plant new flowers
                you don't own me

I reach out for the children
        their sunflower faces
                sacrifice the weak

stretch my bleeding arms over the wall
        with my breathing mask on
                live free or die

my blood is on the petals
        wounds left by the militia
                my body my choice

I wash the flowers with my time
        deadhead them with my sobs
                don't tread on me

dullness flattens my brain but not
        the curve, flowers bloom in the
                fake crisis

Quarantined

Don't slide down that hill
there is nothing at the bottom
nothing
but nothingness
haunting your form
your former form
a skeleton holds you up
as you slide
descend
deploy
deplorable
deep lassitude
your cognition
has no ignition
or initiation

Why

Empaths become
replenished in nature

watching fawns
play with squirrels

while absorbing the losses
of strangers on the news

there is a lot of weeping
for hopeless causes

and *why*
does the world sorrow?

empaths are
unable to build a wall

around their spirit and the horror
of the separated children

but say we should all rage
and ask where are your tears?

Lines

My wall calendar helps me to visualize
my life, the plans I hold dear, the people
I must see so they also see me

At first the lines were through the
scribbling on my calendar, an oddity
disappointing at most—a temporary month

Sometimes there were two lines
an X-ing out, a permanent loss
I catalogued the failures in my diary

Then the lines were of standing humans
waiting to vote, car-lines of hungry children
waiting for the food their school had denied them

lines circling the parking lots for tests
lines at the border, lines at the shelters
lines at the unemployment office

lines in the streets to confront the wizard
behind the curtain asking *when we will be normal?*
But he was a fraud, a canceler of science, of truth

Freedom was not taken by a government
freedom was not taken at all, only
innocent lives, their coffins in orderly lines

The lines are now for a miracle
for we who are left, whose lives have not
been crossed out, who are free to live

I, WASP

I am not a peripheral
nor illegal human being

my flesh, the churchgoing
does not make me America, never has

since native tribes
thrived on their land

long before us
farming without raping the soil

cherishing the buffalo
before the malicious slaughter

my origin story is a perk
of present and past necessities

everything earned
had a kickstarter campaign

every move had a living hope
a paper trail of sponsors

I am not invisible
nor silenced

you have heard my voice
the hymn singing, the poems

you have seen
the job offers, mortgaged houses

you may have noticed the low hurdles
you may have wondered why

Incantation

Oh smothering summer
with your contagion and sweat,

take your infectious mildew
and shove it into the white hot sky,

plunge it into the bilious earth
and sanitize our clotted viral air.

All you give is poisonous ivy
and multitudes of basking larvae

lurking in my lungs and crawling across
my bifurcated skin like an infection.

Succulents love you, but I hate your
enclosures and zooming machines,

I hate your reports— your moist, adhesive
nineties, your worsening statistics.

Come glowing leaves and touch my fevered brow,
come cool gatherings and healing nights.

Come new year and be better than the last,
let it be nothing but a bad dream.

The Praying Mantis

my ramparts
are weakening
in this dysphoria
i'm trying to come back
but my brain is too heavy
today
i can hold a bullet
but not the gun
so my visions are as useless
as a border wall
but the praying mantis
that dropped
from the sky
gave me hope
she stayed the night
blurred into the
greenery at my side
while we prayed together
she was beautiful
and motionless as I was all that day
and into the next twilight

Apart

I miss the singers,
how we stitched black marks together

to make a memory quilt,
where the songs are hidden in the folds.

I long for the light-energy
soaring through the glass,

walking into God's morning hands
like candles on Christmas Eve.

I hunger for the weapon of travel,
how we once defended ourselves

with magical thinking and so
little imagination.

I thirst like a dusty river
for the onus of responsibility

and order, the tasks of joining,
the real-time sounds of humanity.

I pine for the children,
their weight and pull as I push

the swing, our fingers in the clay,
their hands in mine.

Sound

I fall in love with today
with the dog barking at nothing
and the tea kettle screaming

I fall in love with the clattering
in the basement and the wind
brushing the leaves in the trees

I fall in love with music
that emits its gifts from every
small machine in my possession

I fall in love with the hum
of the overfed refrigerator
and the ping of the dryer

I fall in love with the same
voice I hear every day
every year, all these years

the pop of logs in the fireplace
the soft rush of air from the mattress

the sound of lips pulling together
and apart again

Ascension

The bird lifts its wings like a conductor
as I stay flat
although my insides are unruly
heaving with a desire to fly
I didn't sing for the birds today
or the day before
the verdancy outside the window
is momentarily gone
in this brief confused season
the wind blows the snow
off of the pale new leaves
as I read his manuscript
and it is so much better than mine
I look at photos
the child took of me in the terrible light
then delete my broken capillaries
erase the diminishment and scourge
no longer a harbinger   I am here now
the little girls didn't care
they hung from my neck when I arrived
and cried when I left
I felt their mother
being pulled out of my body
as I drove home
in the car I tried to sing all the songs
I've ever sung but they are now inaudible
lost in the archives of time

so I must praise that I am alive
after a year of death
ante up my soul
like yesterday
and lift wings

In the Center

What I mean when I say heart
is not the pulsing muscle

but how you twist mine
and wring it out

with just the face and voice
God gave you

I watch you change from week to week
shape-shifting and learning love

forgiving all of us our daily
failures and missteps

reminding us of what is in the middle
of this life, this constant vibration

this turning and holding
like the one last leaf hanging

on to a tiny twig in the winds
of a bleak midwinter night

Plenty

out of the window
the one I gaze through
in this writing room
I cannot contain
what I see in the yard
the daily creation story
there just for me
the bluebirds have returned
and I stop again and again
to take in the complimentary
colors   like the sky flying by
each time I am like a child
in that first glorious moment
on Christmas morning finding
the stocking Santa filled while
I was asleep   each morning
holds a new treasure   I am
surrounded by revelations,
the cosmos, the masterpiece
it is enough for me
it is enough for the day

Emergence

don't mistake these walls for your prison
        give it a second chance a hope

tumble through the silence
        and come out into your muses

they are still under the pink
        it will be like stepping out of a Renoir

all pale pastels and bathing girls
        curved edges with no sharps

your feet will move like honey
        your eyes will turn to the sky

you were not alone all of these
        viral weeks and empty nights

be a window and crawl out into
        the universe healing and breathing

into the straw fields where
        the children have been dancing

the newborns have been weaning
        we have been waiting for your arrival

for your long lovely embrace

After This

After this I will meet you in the sunlight,
        our skirts twirling, with shoes we never wear.

After this spell is broken we will build a pyre out
        of the foxy dross of lies and glow like the embers.

We will listen to the children, standing on our tiptoes
        to better hear their judgement and their destiny.

After this marauder crawls out of town on its knees,
        we will ride chariots of fire, climb ladders to the sky

to bury the contamination and calamity of our confinement,
        and while we are closer to God we will pray for justice.

After this holy war is over we will kick off our shoes
        and wear our release as a cloak of survival.

v.

Let Love and Faithfulness never leave you; bind them around your neck, write them on the tablet of your heart.

-Proverbs 3:3

Collective

In this dry desert of a day
I love you

like the galaxy of stars
over the Grand Canyon

as entangled as a
bed of snakes

a cloud of bats,
a rumpus of baboons

you alight in me like
a murmuration of starlings

arriving at a surprise party
blanketing the frozen grass

in a melee of deafening desire
as brilliant as a muster of peacocks

Torn Heart

It's not too late to unscar yourself
from when you were a hummingbird wing
and everything tore at your delicacy.

Time is like an ex-lover you
learned to hate but you may still hold
pressed into your closed fist.

The past is a bully,
an afterimage of injustice,
a militia encroaching,

but there is a battlefield where
blood has seeped into the ground
and flowers have bloomed above.

There is an hour when you will let
your hummingbird wounds go,
and you will pause at the beauty of your life.

Sublime

Long ago I dreamed of a soul consciousness
and God never made it easier to find,

the world is covered in words and labels,
the illusions are the great heartbreak.

But there is a sublimity
in disentangling from the past

which is gone from existence
except in the choice to resurrect it.

On our islands we named it
and believed in our pitiful understanding,

suffering was the choice,
to prove instead of improve,

like a game of telephone, talking and time
distorted and removed so much good, but

love remained; a remnant, but still present,
and there is nothing that cannot be healed by love.

Another Day

The ant is carrying a seed four times
his size across the rail of my deck.

Ten minutes later he's rounded
the corner four feet away.

I could flick him off, but I wonder
where he is going, and, if he makes it

to the end of the rail by dark,
does he consider it a productive day?

I am reading, but distracted by his progress.
I move a potted plant to let him by and see

that there are dozens of seeds hidden beneath the pot.
I have the power to wipe his world away

with the swish of my hand, like an ant tsunami,
an insect earthquake, a bug hurricane.

He is toiling away in futility as I look down
in my omnipotence,

just as, I am sure, God is looking down
at me on this wasted day.

Gratitude

God is already in you, born in you
waiting for you to say yes

yes to the ineffable sea
and the mountains pulled out of the earth

yes to the abundance of the day
and the pulse of your heart

to be possessed in thanksgiving
and all that is good and right

to invoke grace and reject fear
in reverence of life itself

throw your eyes to the sky
and feel the waterfall inside you

verdant and flowing with
no beginning and no end

turn toward the sun and simply
say thank you every day

for we choose our path to gratitude
and in gratitude we learn peace

Meditation

I am breathing for you now,
the ocean in the back of my throat.

My prayer hands at soul center,
holding you, keeping you there.

My bones lengthen and stretch,
the heart opens and rises toward heaven.

In the turnings of this life there is one
who will never leave you.

On days when you are trying to breath
and be loved all at the same time

let my arms ease your pain,
let my sorrow join yours.

United in our rarefied place,
from here I can see oblivion, but

in this house of broken hearts,
in the land of the living,

God is hidden in the rafters
quiet, still, on every silent night.

Final Flight
(for Louie)

When wings expand at last, each of us
will have one singular moment:
airborn, lifting free, voiceless.
We are made for final flight.

In this time between flights,
theirs and ours,
we wait out the unanswered days,
our senses permanently altered,

gliding through dreams and daydreams
tendrils of a spirit entwining us,
yoking us, so close
to the line we cannot cross.

Our hearts float in their own seas,
alone, searching for the voyager
who has crossed the uncrossable line
and left us behind.

Memories relentlessly skimming the edges
of our brains, sheathing themselves in eternity,
while ordinary life goes on
outside our earthly windows.

But someday the veil will be lifted
and we will be invited to the party
in the unknown Kingdom
in joyful reunion with our Maker.

Now we hold each other in broken arms,
we lift each other in hopeful prayers,
until we take our final glorious flight
away from the rabble of this known world.

Until We Meet Again
(for my cousins)

An ordinary day, an ordinary freshwater beach
the breeze slaps at my skin
the clouds curl and twist above
the sun already blotching my shoulders

as I ungracefully lug the necessities of the day
through the stony gray sand
I glance to the east at the grove of trees
sheltering the elderly picnic tables

and my soul sees a group of people
sharing food, laughing, talking
children are nearby digging in the sand
kites and frisbees fly by

moms fix sandwiches and wash sandy hands
dads carry little ones towards the water
grandparents envelop babies on their laps
there are aunts, uncles, cousins

and there are so many angels

I am overcome with their presence
sudden tears wash over my face
it's not a memory or a mirage
I can see them—I can see us—all of us

throughout the day I turn from the water
to look back and we are still there
but today the reunion is only in my heart
until we meet again

The Speaker

The popular speaker attracts a crowd everywhere he goes and his followers on social media grow exponentially. He doesn't need to advertise—old-fashioned word-of-mouth seems to do the trick. They like his style, his laid-back manner, the relatable stories he tells.

The noise of the throng hushes as he starts to speak—it's magical, like a miracle that anyone would take this seriously with the abundance of phonies out there peddling their conspiracy theories——but they stay, they listen, they believe.

Sometimes the stories are a bit cryptic and the fans don't always understand (so later they will form small discussion groups to share ideas). They claim it's life-changing, like a good self-help book. If only he'd write this stuff down it would be a best seller, they say.

But one day the crowd gets restless. Some protesters start a chant. The people are tired and hungry since the speech that day had been an extra long one. The speaker does not look concerned. He raises his hand to quiet the crowd and says the solution is very simple. Share what you have, give freely, and there will be enough for everyone— no questions asked—no miracle needed.

Simple Stories

Adam and Eve taught us that
we have freedom to choose, but

Noah's ark showed us that sometimes
God is disappointed in our choices.

Jonah in the whale revealed we
should not ignore a second chance.

The prodigal son gave us reassurance
that we can come home again, and when

thousands were hungry, Jesus taught
them how to share what they had.

The story of Mary and Martha
reminded us to just listen sometimes,

and the good Samaritan showed us
that everyone is worthy of help.

Zacchaeus was despised but Jesus
ate dinner with him, loved him anyway.

Jesus walked on water, showing us
He can calm any storm, and when

He healed the leper He defied the law,
so we know that love always comes first.

When He said: Do not judge, or
you, too, will be judged, He meant it.

When He hung on the cross He
demonstrated that anyone can be forgiven.

Ebb and Flow

What if God is love
and that is all there is to it?

He is not an entity, a thing,
but a human experience

embodied in a name
we can understand

we give him a pronoun,
a title, attributes and glory

we place him in a house
that we visit from time to time

we celebrate his victories
and defeats with immutable

traditions, meaningless to many
that ebb and flow with the emotion

of the moment, with our
willingness, our mood

what if he is not a member
of your church, does not live

in a book or the music
but just in you.

These Children

These children were not born of me
but are in me, part of me. I am a part of them
in blood and ineffable love.

These children have me
in common, the one who appears at the door,
the one they recognize together,

the one who would swim to them day or night,
in floodwaters, in muck or mud, treading
water, paddling against a current of wind,

or climbing a mountain of stone just to hear
their exclamations, to see their flawless
beauty, to provide my soul assurance

in their awareness of me, my adoration
of them, to hear the galloping of my heart,
to sit with me while they will.

Why We Are Here

My awareness opens likes leaves on
the first warm day of May with

so much assuredness that life will
go on, despite the sunless chill

of the months gone by.
Where there was a vacancy,

there is something added, something
to help us carry on and remember

why we are here, to be ambitious in
tomorrow, to praise the stardust

and its Maker, and all who went
before us. Like graffiti on our skin

we can plainly see the truth. We visit
the garden and notice the flowers

have colors we have never seen, stems
that have expanded overnight.

It all happens frighteningly fast,
this breathing from sunlight

to moonlight, this every day
with its time, obsolete and everlasting

at the same moment, these babies
who keep coming into their beauty.

Diane Vogel Ferri is a teacher, poet, and writer living in Solon, Ohio. Her latest novel is No Life But This: A Novel of Emily Warren Roebling. Her essays have been published in *Scene Magazine, Yellow Arrow Journal, Cleveland Christmas Memories,Good Works Review,* and by *Cleveland State University* among others. Her poems can be found in numerous journals such as *Wend Poetry, Rubbertop Review, American Journal of Poetry,* and *Poet Lore*. Her previous publications are: *Liquid Rubies* (poetry), *The Volume of Our Incongruity* (poetry), and *The Desire Path* (novel). Diane's essay, "I Will Sing for You" was featured at the Cleveland Humanities Festival in 2018.

www.ingramcontent.com/pod-product-compliance
Lightning Source LLC
Chambersburg PA
CBHW030333100526
44592CB00010B/686